DC SECRETS REVEALED!

BEHIND THE SCENES WITH
BATMAN

by Steve Korté

Batman created by Bob Kane with Bill Finger

a Capstone company — publishers for children

Raintree is an imprint of Capstone Global Library Limited, a company incorporated in England and Wales having its registered office at 264 Banbury Road, Oxford, OX2 7DY – Registered company number: 6695582

www.raintree.co.uk
myorders@raintree.co.uk

Copyright © 2025 DC.
BATMAN and all related characters and elements © & ™ DC. (s25)

All rights reserved. No part of this publication may be reproduced in any form or by any means (including photocopying or storing it in any medium by electronic means and whether or not transiently or incidentally to some other use of this publication) without the written permission of the copyright owner, except in accordance with the provisions of the Copyright, Designs and Patents Act 1988 or under the terms of a licence issued by the Copyright Licensing Agency, 5th Floor, Shackleton House, 4 Battle Bridge Lane, London SE1 2HX (www.cla.co.uk). Applications for the copyright owner's written permission should be addressed to the publisher.

ISBN 978 1 3982 5696 5 (hardback)

Editorial Credits
Edited by Christopher Harbo
Designed by Sarah Bennett
Production by Katy LaVigne
Printed and bound in India

Acknowledgements
We would like to thank the following for permission to reproduce photographs: Design Elements by Shutterstock/mei yanotai (folder), 18, 19, Shutterstock/Mikhail Grachikov (grid background), 13, 14

British Library Cataloguing in Publication Data
A full catalogue record for this book is available from the British Library.

Contents

Meet Batman. 4

The man behind the mask 6

The Batcave. 8

Powers and skills. 10

The ultimate Utility Belt 12

Batman's vehicles 14

Awesome allies .16

Secrets of the Super-Villains 20

Team player. 28

    Historical highlights of
    the Caped Crusader. 30

    About the author. 32

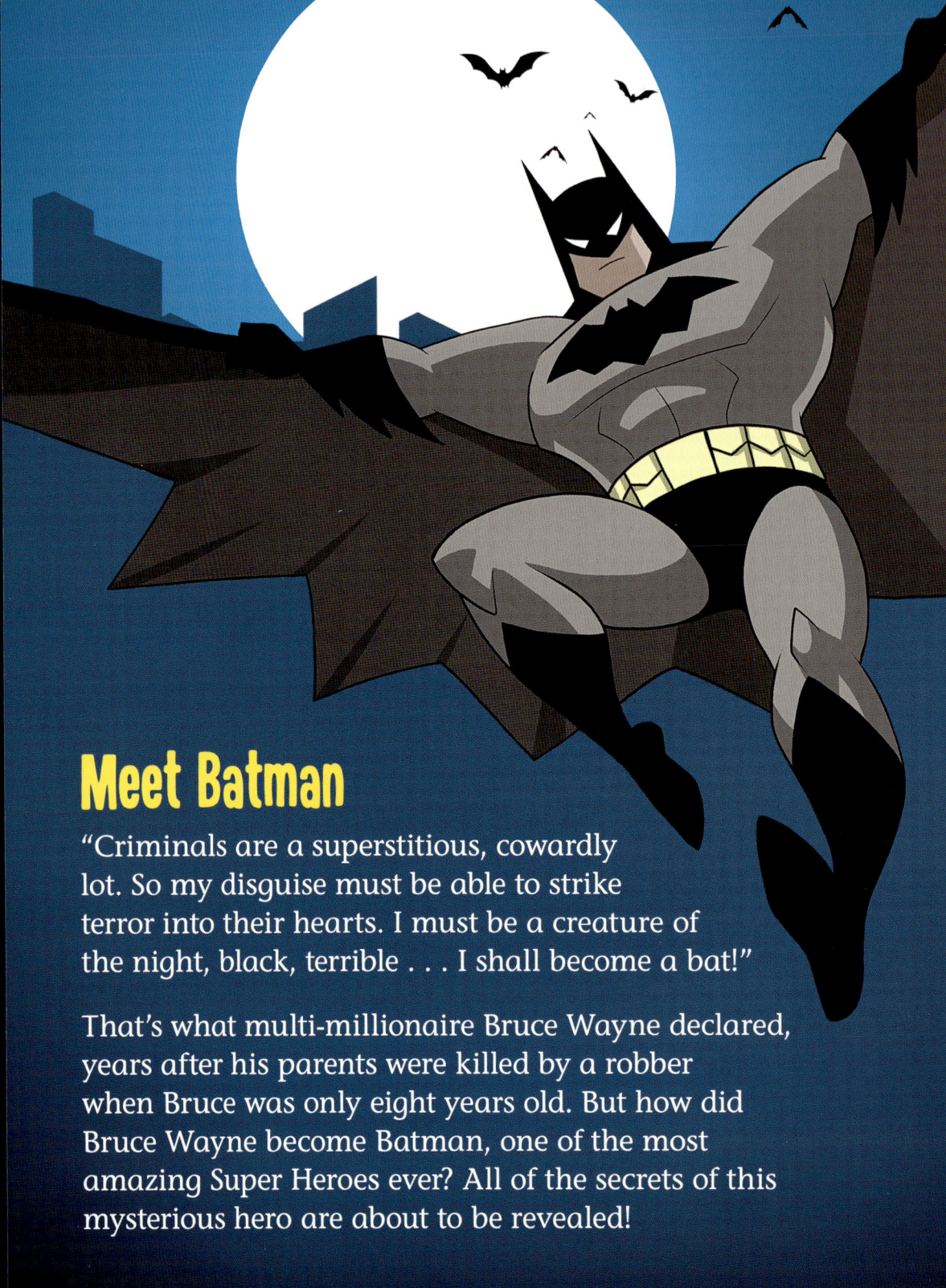

Meet Batman

"Criminals are a superstitious, cowardly lot. So my disguise must be able to strike terror into their hearts. I must be a creature of the night, black, terrible . . . I shall become a bat!"

That's what multi-millionaire Bruce Wayne declared, years after his parents were killed by a robber when Bruce was only eight years old. But how did Bruce Wayne become Batman, one of the most amazing Super Heroes ever? All of the secrets of this mysterious hero are about to be revealed!

Batman's many nicknames

The Dark Knight

The Caped Crusader

Gotham City's Guardian

The World's Greatest Detective

Who cares about Batman's nicknames? Mine are so much better!

The Clown Prince of Crime!

The Ace of Knaves!

The Harlequin of Hate!

HA HA HA HA!!

The man behind the mask

When he was young, Bruce Wayne made a vow to fight crime. He began travelling the world, learning martial arts and other fighting skills.

He also studied science and learned from the best police detectives. When he returned from his journey, he was ready to become Batman.

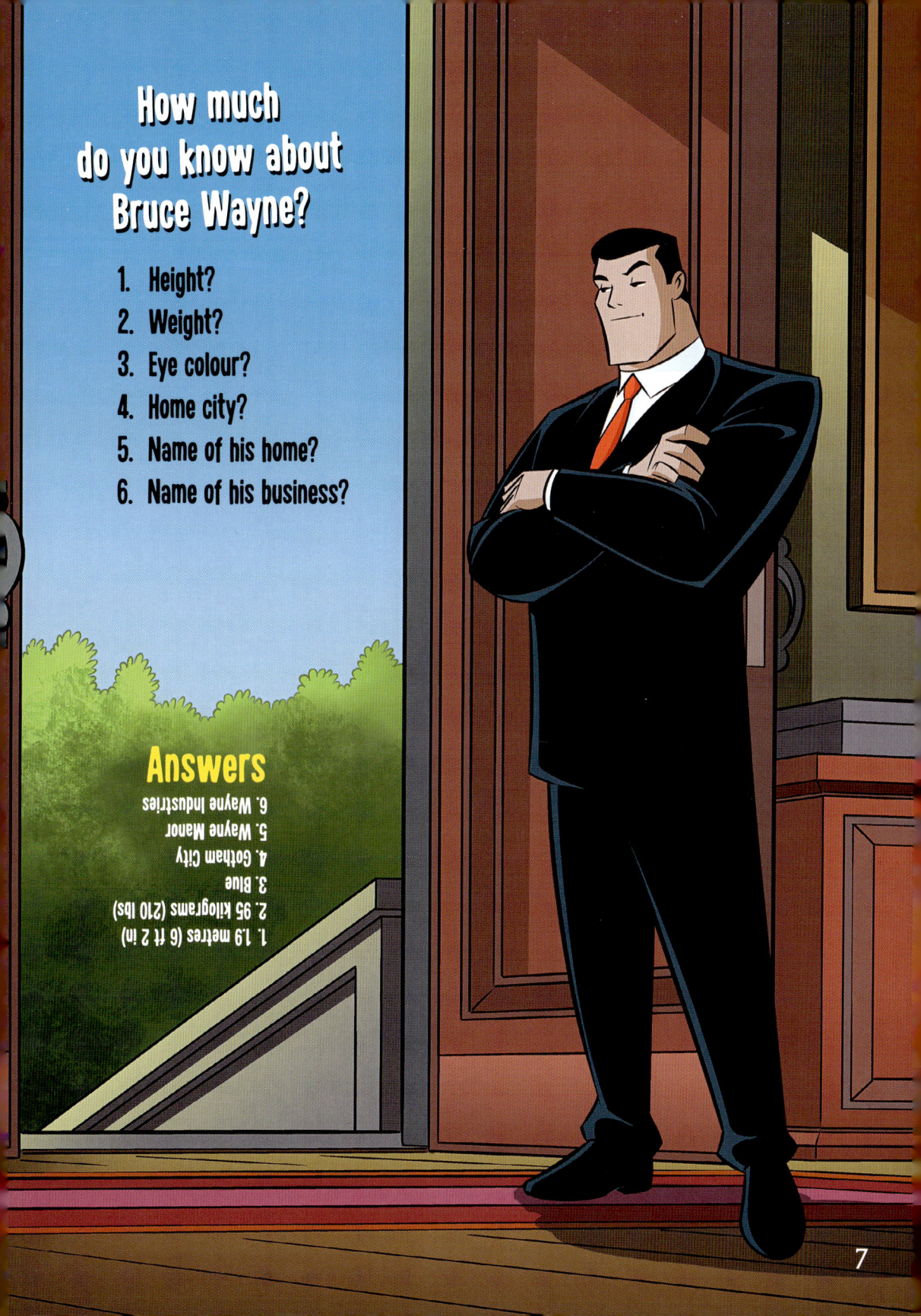

How much do you know about Bruce Wayne?

1. Height?
2. Weight?
3. Eye colour?
4. Home city?
5. Name of his home?
6. Name of his business?

Answers
1. 1.9 metres (6 ft 2 in)
2. 95 kilograms (210 lbs)
3. Blue
4. Gotham City
5. Wayne Manor
6. Wayne Industries

The Batcave

Bruce Wayne was a young boy when he accidentally tumbled into a cave far beneath Wayne Manor. That cave is now Batman's secret headquarters. The Batcave contains everything Batman needs to fight his war on crime: a state-of-the-art Batcomputer, several vehicles, a science lab and a gym.

Hall of Trophies

A section of the Batcave contains souvenirs from some of Batman's most famous cases, including the following items:

- A life-size robot of a Tyrannosaurus rex that came from Gotham City's Dinosaur Island amusement park
- A huge playing card from one of The Joker's crimes

10:47
Many years ago, Bruce Wayne's parents were killed at 10:47 p.m. Today, there is a grandfather clock in Wayne Manor. When Bruce moves the clock's hands to 10:47, a panel in the wall slides open to reveal a secret entry to the Batcave.

- A giant 1947 penny that was used by the villainous Penny Plunderer
- A two-headed silver dollar used by Two-Face
- One of The Penguin's trick umbrellas

Powers and skills

Although Batman has no superpowers, he does have incredible strength and amazing crime-fighting tools. He also trains every day in his gym in the Batcave. This is just one page of his training schedule:

MONDAY EVENING

Weight lifting: 120 kg, 8 sets of 3 reps each

Metabolic conditioning: 5 sets, each including:

    1/2-kilometre run

    21 kettlebell swings

    12 pull-ups

Flexibility: 30 minutes

Sparring: 30 minutes

TUESDAY MORNING

Jogging: 30 minutes

Meditation: 30 minutes

Metabolic conditioning: 5 sets, each including:

    6-metre rope climb

    10 high box jumps

    50 crunches

Heavy punching bag: 30 minutes

Batarang target practice: 30 minutes

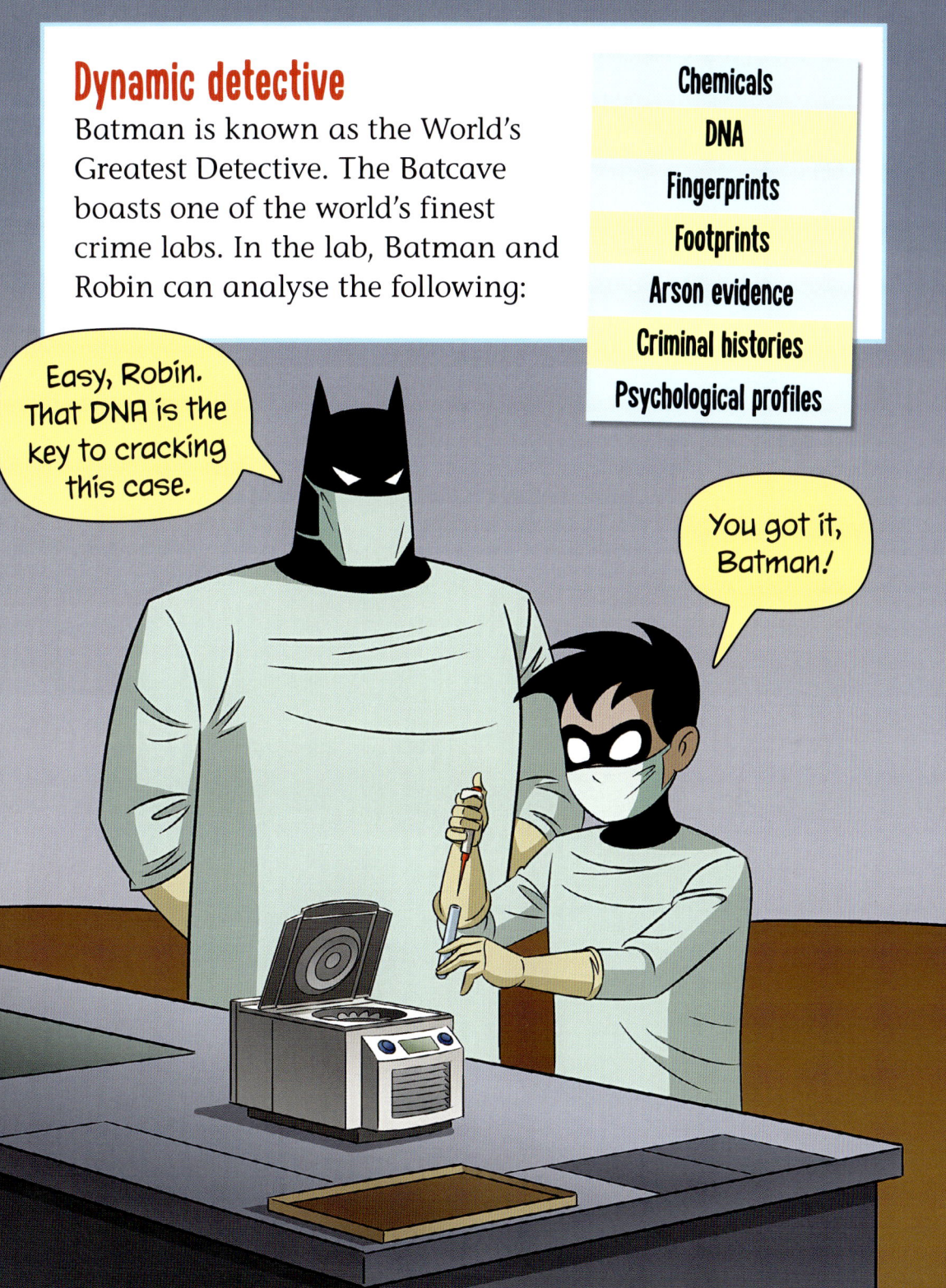

The ultimate Utility Belt

Batman's yellow Utility Belt is filled with dozens of crime-fighting tools. Here are just a few of the top-secret gadgets hidden inside its pouches:

- ✔ Batrope
- ✔ Batarangs
- ✔ Tracking device
- ✔ Bat-cuffs
- ✔ Torch
- ✔ Smoke capsules
- ✔ Make-up and disguise kit
- ✔ Flash-bang grenades
- ✔ Fingerprinting kit and DNA analyser

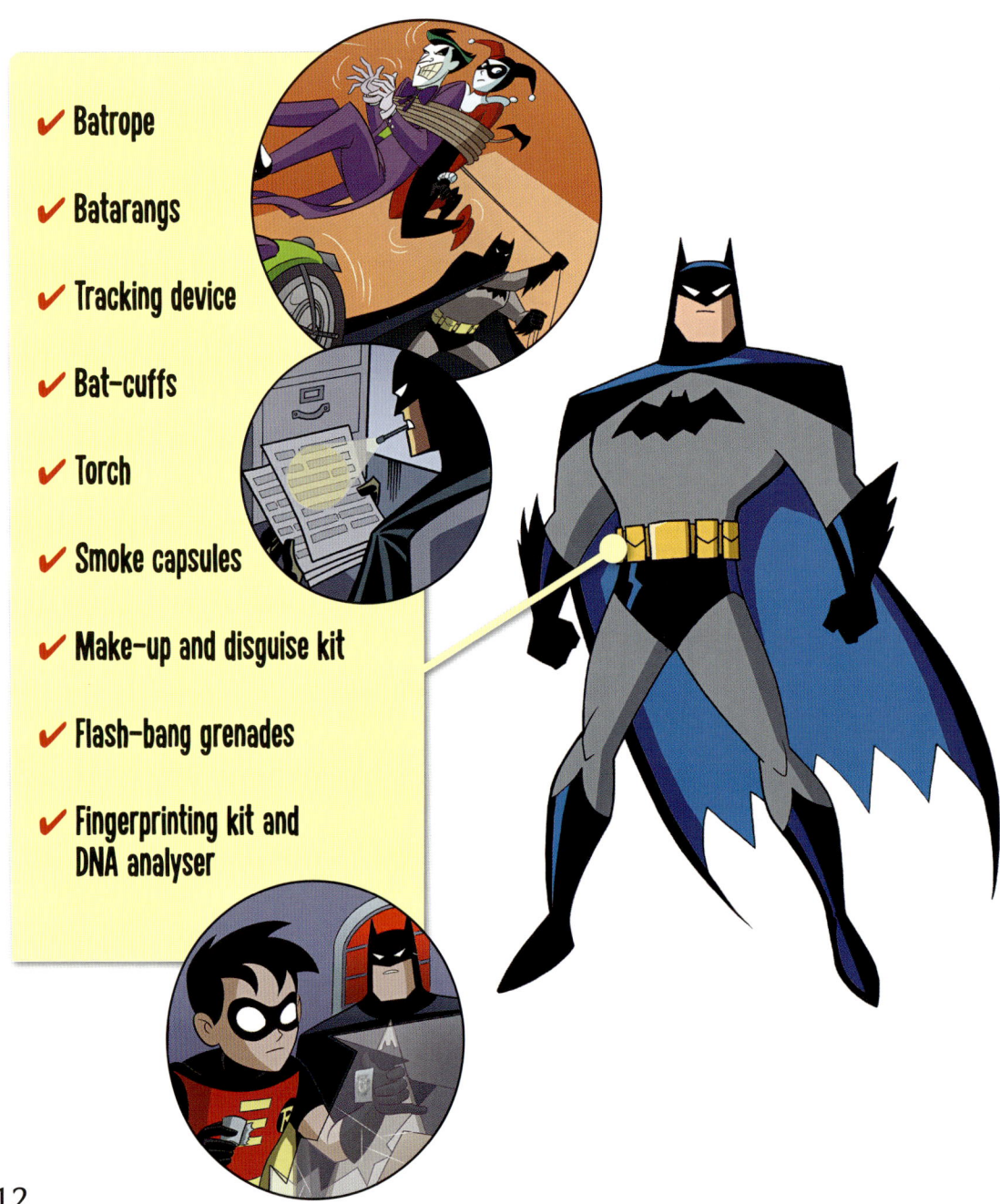

Batarangs

Batman has designed dozens of Batarangs, including:

| Magnet batarangs | Bomb batarangs |
| Seeing-eye batarangs | Harpoon batarangs |

Top 5 odd Utility Belt items

- Shark repellent
- A marble to make footstep sounds when rolled down stairs
- Chemicals to change water into ice
- A lightweight Batsuit
- A Batman hologram projector

Batman's vehicles

Bruce Wayne built the most amazing car in the world: the Batmobile! This awesome automobile is jet-powered and as strong as a tank. A few of its hidden features include:

- Jet turbine
- Rocket-fired ejector seats
- Crime lab
- Radar screen
- Chemical blackout fog
- Sticky foam launcher
- Armour plating
- Reinflatable tyres
- Rocket-fired grappling hook
- 1200 horsepower engine
- Advanced radar jamming device

Land, air and sea vehicles

The Batmobile rules the streets of Gotham City, but here are just a few of Batman's other crime-fighting vehicles:

- Batboat
- Bat-Copter
- Bat-Rocket
- Batcycle
- Batgyro
- Batplane
- Bat-Raptor

Awesome allies

Batman doesn't always fight crime alone. Here are just a few of his friends, teammates and allies.

Alfred Pennyworth

When Bruce Wayne became an orphan, his family's butler, Alfred, became a father figure to him. Alfred is now an important part of Batman's crime-fighting operation. He even helped to design and sew an early version of Batman's uniform.

Alfred,

Sorry the material is so difficult to work with, but I think we are on the right track. This is heavy-duty material that should protect me from bullets and sharp objects. Of course, that is why you are having so much trouble making alterations to it.

One minor detail: Can you maybe make the "ears" longer? It could help scare some criminals.

— Bruce

Commissioner Gordon

Along with Alfred, Gotham City's Police Commissioner, James Gordon, has long been an ally to Batman. He often summons the hero by lighting the Bat-Signal on top of the police headquarters.

The Bat-Signal
The Bat-Signal has bulletproof glass to protect its lens. It also has a fog-filter that allows it to penetrate thick fog and smoke.

Robin
Real name: Tim Drake

Nickname: Boy Wonder

Height: 1.6 metres (5 ft 5 in)

Weight: 56 kg (125 lbs)

Hair: Black

Utility Belt: Batarangs, Batropes, gas capsules and more

Team leader: Teen Titans

Batwing

Batwing is really Luke Fox, a former boxer and brilliant scientist. His high-tech uniform has even more features than Batman's Batsuit.

- Mask to conceal identity
- Power of flight
- Power of super-strength
- Super-strong fabric that withstands laser rays
- Built-in computer system

SECRET FILE

Batgirl

- Secret identity is Barbara Gordon, Commissioner Gordon's daughter
- Has outstanding computer skills
- Became Batgirl to clear her father's name for a crime he didn't commit
- Is a superb martial artist
- Batman knows her true identity, but her father does not

Ace the Bat-Hound: The World's Greatest Dog Detective

- Cowl to mask true identity
- Ultra-hearing
- Bat-Symbol
- Powerful paws
- Utility Collar with high-tech gadgets
- Fireproof cape

Batwoman

SECRET FILE

- Real Name: Katherine "Kate" Kane
- Eyes: Blue
- Hair: Red
- Uniform: Impact-resistant fabric
- Boots: Steel-toed

Nightwing

Richard "Dick" Grayson was a child acrobat at Haly's Circus. Batman trained him to become the first Robin. Years later, Dick started fighting crime as Nightwing.

Secrets of the Super-Villains

Gotham City has some of the scariest villains on Earth. How much do you really know about them? Dive into the secrets about each foe pulled from the Batcomputer's files!

The Joker

The Clown Prince of Crime is Batman's most dangerous enemy. But did you know . . .

- The Joker's hair turned permanently green after he fell into a vat of chemicals.

- If The Joker has a flower tucked into his coat pocket, be careful! It often squirts deadly gas or liquids.

- Watch out for his Joker Venom! One drop of it forces his victims to smile and laugh for hours.

- Every part of The Joker's outfit is dangerous. The toes of his shoes contain pop-out weapons.

The Penguin's secret origin story

Oswald Chesterfield Cobblepot grew up with no friends except for the birds in his mother's pet shop. He was a strange-looking child, with a sharp beak nose and a waddling walk. Other children nicknamed him "Penguin". When some bullies damaged Mrs Cobblepot's pet shop, Oswald became enraged and began a life of crime as The Penguin.

Catching the Penguin

The Penguin has a special umbrella that shoots a sticky pink goo. One time, Batman turned the umbrella around and used it to trap the villain with his own weapon.

What do you get when a dinosaur crashes cars?

Answer: Tyrannosaurus Wrecks

The Riddler's first crime

When Edward Nigma was a young boy, his history teacher announced a competition to see who could put together a jigsaw puzzle the fastest. The night before the competition, Nigma broke into his teacher's desk and took a photo of the assembled puzzle. The next morning, he won the competition because he knew what the finished puzzle looked like.

Poison Ivy

Psychological fun facts

Real name is Pamela Isley

One of the world's best botanists

Prefers plants to people

Would rather feed you to her giant Venus fly trap than say good morning

Two-Face

Two-Face got his name after one half of his face became scarred by chemicals. Two-Face's crimes always involve the number two. Here are a few of his famous crimes:

- Robbing the audience attending a performance of Brahms' Double Concerto
- Stealing two rare books of Shakespeare plays
- Robbing the spectators at a doubles tennis match
- Holding the employees of a firm hostage on the 22nd floor of a Gotham City skyscraper

Bane

The massive Super-Villain Bane gets his strength from a chemical called Venom. Tubes pump the dangerous chemical directly into his bloodstream. In one of Batman's most vicious battles, Bane broke Batman's back.

Felonious fact
Bane has been declared dead several times. But each time he has returned stronger and more dangerous than before.

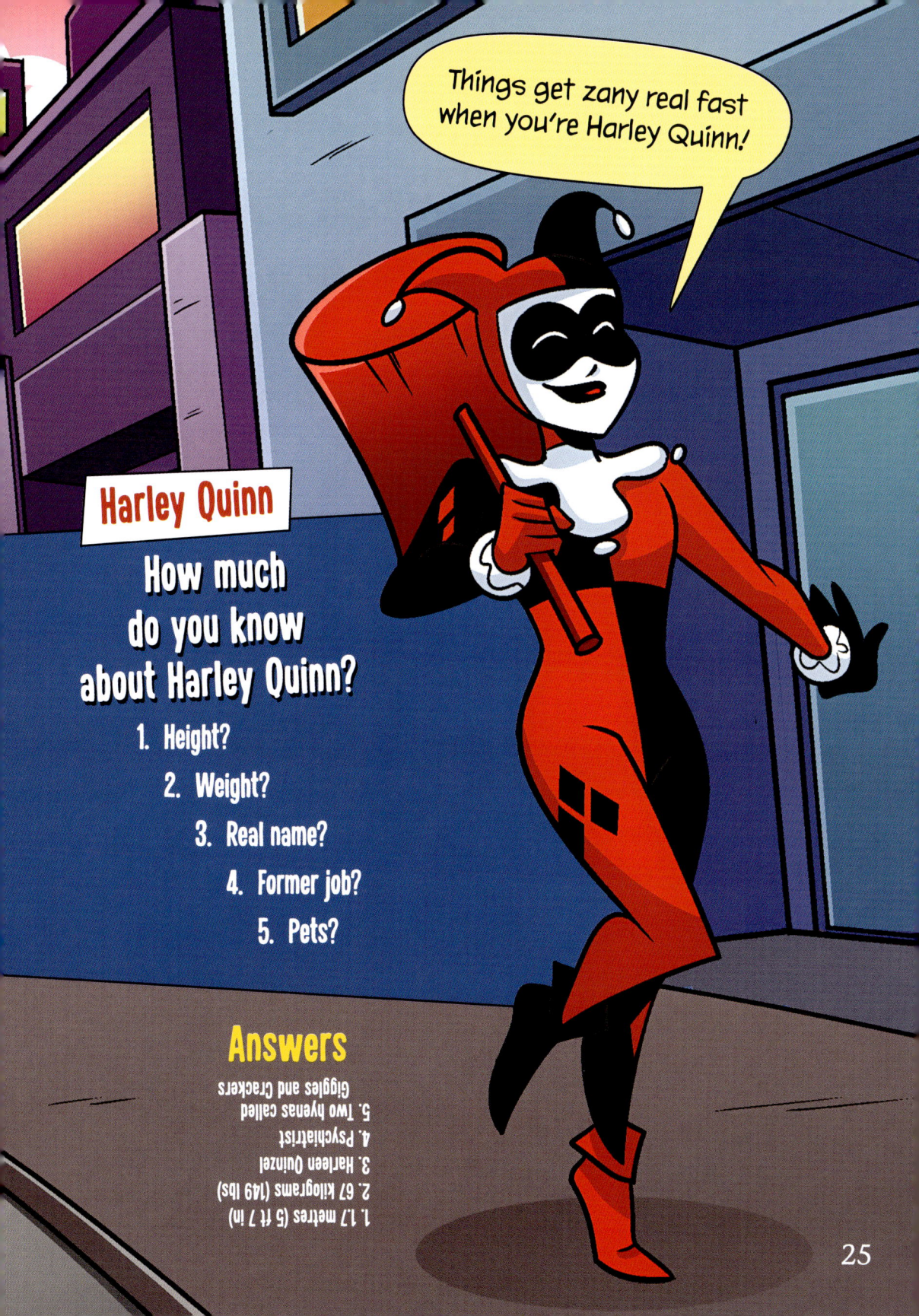

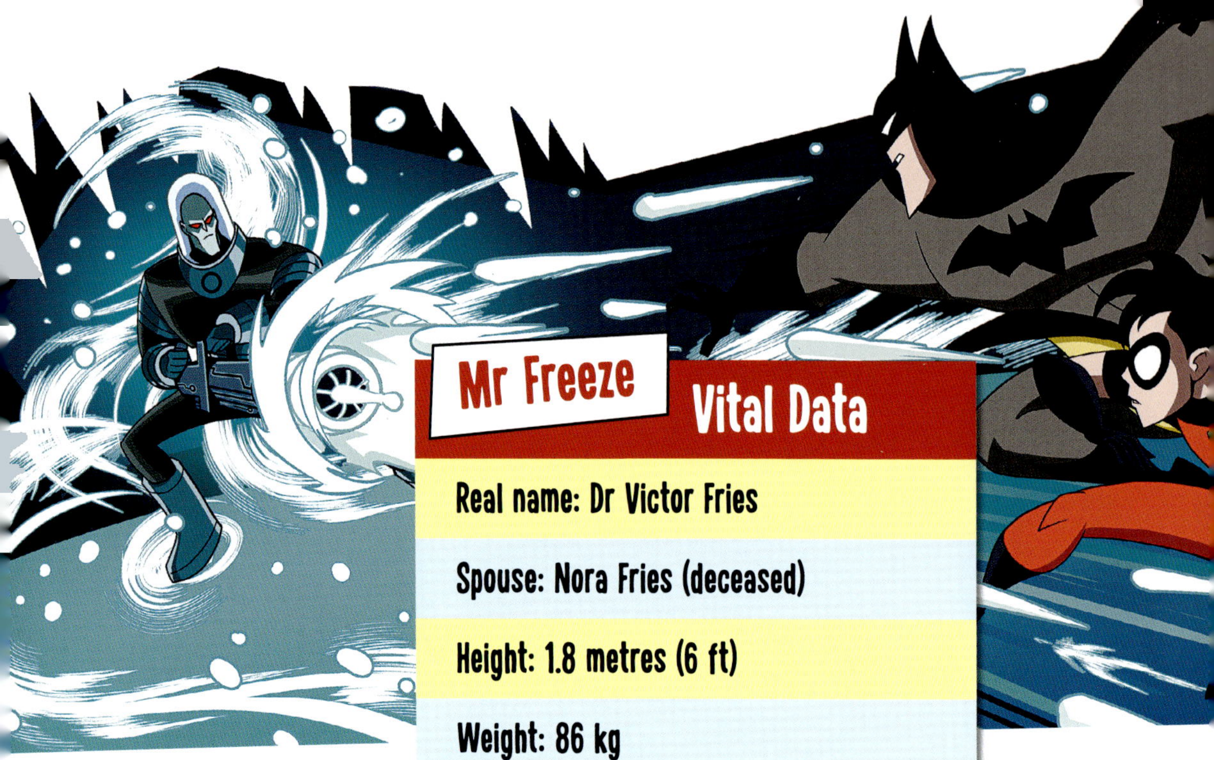

Mr Freeze

Vital Data

Real name: Dr Victor Fries

Spouse: Nora Fries (deceased)

Height: 1.8 metres (6 ft)

Weight: 86 kg

Outfit: Air-conditioned suit of armour that never goes above freezing point

Favourite weapon: Ice-blasting freeze ray

Killer Croc

- Waylon Jones (real name)
- 2.2 metres (7 ft 5 in) tall
- 311 kilograms (686 lbs)
- Red eyes
- Scaly skin caused by a genetic mutation
- Began his career wrestling alligators in a travelling carnival

Clayface

There have been several Clayface villains. One was a film star called Matt Hagen, who started using a dangerous mud-like facial cream. When a criminal forced him to consume an entire barrel of the cream, it took over Hagen's body. It gave him the power to transform into almost anything. His many talents include:

- Changing his arms and hands into spikes, hammers and blades
- Absorbing items and changing his body to match them
- Extending his limbs for long distances
- Dissolving his body into a puddle and disappearing into the sewers

Team player

Batman is a founder member of the Justice League, a team of the world's most powerful heroes. He is one of the few non-superhuman heroes to join the group. The Dark Knight has also partnered up with Superman, Wonder Woman and even a certain cowardly canine and his crew!

Wonder Woman

Batman and Wonder Woman have joined forces to fight crime many times, but their methods don't always match. She is an optimist who tries to end conflicts peacefully. He is a pessimist who never hesitates to use force.

Superman

Clark Kent and Bruce Wayne first met when they were forced to share a very small cabin on a cruise ship. Their close quarters made it difficult for them to hide their secret identities when a fire broke out on the ship. As both jumped into action, their roles as Superman and Batman were revealed to each other.

Scooby-Doo and the Mystery Inc. gang

Scooby-Doo and the Mystery Inc. gang have been solving mysteries and fighting monsters for years. But sometimes they need a little help. Batman, Robin and Ace are always happy to lend a hand . . . or a paw. Scooby-Doo denies the rumour that he is secretly jealous of Ace's detecting skills.

Historical highlights of the Caped Crusader

- In 1938, DC Comics was looking for a new Super Hero. A cartoonist called Bob Kane met up with his writer friend Bill Finger in Poe Park in New York City, USA. Kane, with the help of Finger, worked out the details of a new hero called The Batman.

- The first Batman story was published in *Detective Comics No.27*, which hit newsstands in 1939.

- A copy of *Detective Comics No.27* sold for £1.37 million in 2022.

- Robin the Boy Wonder made his debut in *Detective Comics No.38* in 1940. DC Comics agreed to try out Robin for just one issue. They were worried about featuring a young person fighting gangsters. But sales doubled on the first issue to feature the Boy Wonder, and he became a permanent partner to Batman.

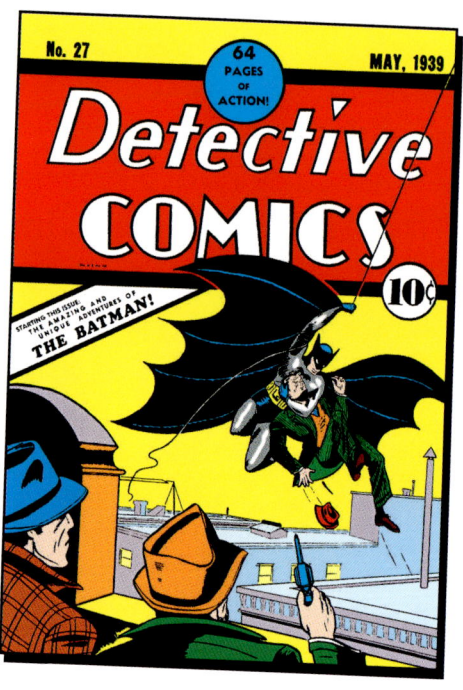

- Batman started appearing in a second comic book in 1940 when *Batman No.1* was published. The Joker and Catwoman, two of Batman's most famous villains, made their first appearances in that issue.

- Batman stories became very unusual during the 1950s. In one strange story, he was transformed into "Zebra Batman", a radioactive, black-and-white-striped menace to the citizens of Gotham City.

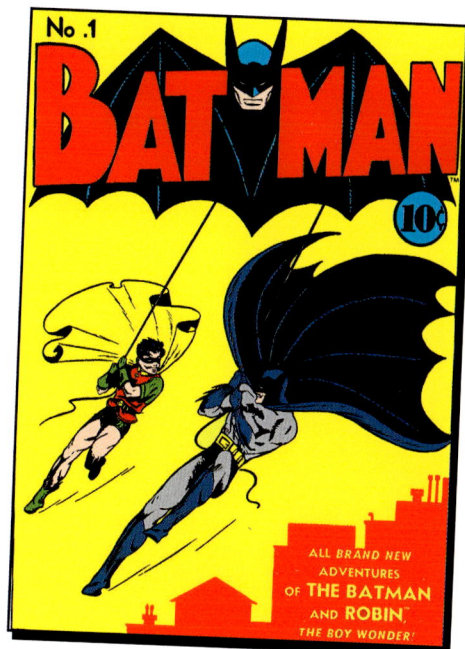

- The *LEGO® Batman Movie* was created by a team of more than 500 people. The amount of time they collectively spent working on the film was equal to 9,153 days. If just one person had been working on the film, it would have taken 25 years to finish it!

- Only two actors have ever won Oscars for their appearances in superhero films, and both of them played The Joker! Heath Ledger won for his role in *The Dark Knight* and Joaquin Phoenix won for his performance in *Joker*.

About the author

Steve Korté is the author of many books for children and young adults. He worked for many years at DC Comics, where he edited more than 600 books about Superman, Batman, Wonder Woman and the other heroes and villains of the DC universe. He lives in New York City, USA, with his husband, Bill, and their super-cat, **Duke**.